Russel Howcroft is one of [illegible] most loved media personalities, and a regular p[illegible]ist on ABC TV's high-rating *Gruen*, hosted by Wil Anderson. He wrote and presented a documentary on Australian advertising legends (and creators of the iconic 'Come on Aussie, come on!' and many more famous jingles) Mo and Jo. He is a Partner and Chief Creative Officer at PwC, the chairman of AFTRS (Australian Film Television and Radio School), a former board member of the Melbourne Football Club and the owner of Caspers – a pie factory in Bayswater, Victoria. Russel's first book, *When it's Right to be Wrong*, was a bestseller for Penguin.

Alex Wadelton is one of Australia's most highly regarded advertising writers and creative directors. In 2016, he was rated as one of the world's top 20 advertising writers. His advertising campaigns have run all around the world. His charity campaigns have raised hundreds of thousands of dollars. And he spearheaded a campaign to create a statue honouring Indigenous footballer Nicky Winmar's iconic stance against racism. *The Right-brain Workout* is his first book.

the right-brain work out

re-train your brain to be more creative in 10 weeks

Russel Howcroft
with **Alex Wadelton**

PENGUIN BOOKS

The information contained in this book is of a general nature only. If you wish to make use of any dietary information in this book relating to your health, you should first consider its appropriateness to your situation, including consulting a medical professional.

PENGUIN

UK | USA | Canada | Ireland | Australia
India | New Zealand | South Africa | China

Penguin is part of the Penguin Random House group of companies whose addresses can be found at global.penguinrandomhouse.com.

Penguin Random House Australia

First published by Penguin Books, 2019

Cover and internal design by Adam Laszczuk © Penguin Random House Australia Pty Ltd
Cover image by erattan/shutterstock.com
Internal images on pages 3, 16, 17, 31, 35, 41, 46, 48, 58, 66, 71, 79, 99, 110 & 116 by shutterstock.com
Printed and bound in China by 1010 Printing International Co Ltd.

NATIONAL LIBRARY OF AUSTRALIA
A catalogue record for this book is available from the National Library of Australia

ISBN 978 1 76089 4955

A proportion of the authors' royalties will be donated to Epilepsy Action Australia.
epilepsy.org.au

Epilepsy Action Australia

penguin.com.au

To all those people who believe in the power of creativity to change the world for the better.

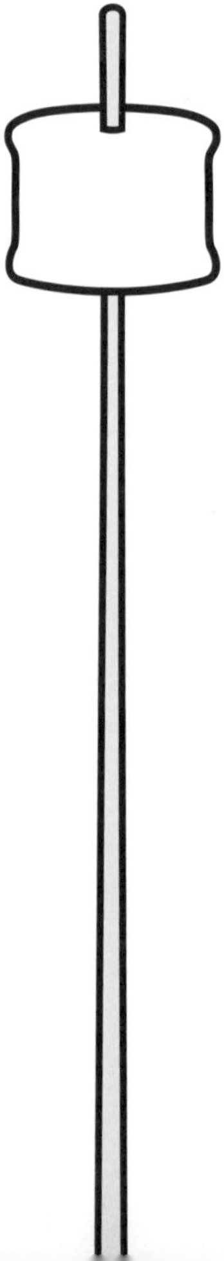

some of you may already know of the Marshmallow Challenge.

The Marshmallow Challenge (not to be confused with the Marshmallow Test) is a simple team-building exercise where groups of four people are asked to build the tallest structure they can out of twenty sticks of spaghetti, a metre of tape, a length of string . . . and a marshmallow.

Designer Tom Wujec conducted research into how different groups perform in the challenge. As he explained in a TED Talk, architects and engineers (thankfully) tend to do well, but one of the worst-performing cohorts is recent graduates of business school.

In observing the different approaches, Wujec thinks part of the problem is that 'business students are trained to find the single right plan'. What tends to happen is they talk about what they're going to do, they jockey for power within the group, they come up with a plan, they 'execute' their plan . . . and then they put the marshmallow on top right at the end.

At this point, more often than not, their structure falls over. Another group that does really well at the Marshmallow Challenge?

kindergarten kids.

Turns out, small children are really good at iterative design. Why? Because they build prototypes as they go, learning lessons and continually integrating these lessons into their work to improve their structure. They naturally collaborate, co-design and co-create – the core pillars of creative learning.

You might also have heard of Dr George Land's research on creativity from the 1960s. Dr Land developed a creativity test for NASA, to help select innovative engineers and scientists.

He identified two types of thinking when it comes to creativity.

Firstly, there's **convergent thinking**, where you judge ideas, criticise them, and refine them.

Secondly, there's **divergent thinking**, where you imagine new ideas: original ones, unique ones and ones which come from the subconscious.

This second one, divergent thinking – the subconscious, the untested, the random association – is true creativity.

It's truly original, lateral and uniquely human. It's the stuff that robots and artificial intelligence simply cannot do.

In 1968, Land started applying his research on creativity to children. He gave his creativity test to 1,600 kids aged from three to five. He then re-tested the same kids at ten years of age, and again at fifteen, and compared their scores against **adults**.

The results were staggering:

98 per cent of five-year-olds were assessed in the 'highly creative' range (at 'genius' level). This dropped to 30 per cent of ten-year-olds. Then just 12 per cent of fifteen-year-olds . . . and only 2 per cent of adults could be considered 'highly creative'.

non-creative thinking, it appears, is a learned behaviour.

And that's why we have written this book. To help you unlearn what you have been taught. Because with *The Right-brain Workout* we are starting out all over again. It's like finger painting for adults. You'll do things you haven't done in years. And you'll rediscover that being creative is a whole lot of fun.

just
imag

ine...

During a blizzard, a giant red koala looks up at a flying washing machine and spontaneously morphs into an old man wearing an armadillo on his head as rainbow-coloured lasers fan out across the night sky.

That sentence makes no sense. But it made you think. It made you imagine it.

And it made you use a part of your brain that we all tend to neglect as we get older and become adults with Terribly Important Responsibilities.

This project is about trying to rediscover the sense of play that we all have when we are kids.

Because when we are children, we make up all sorts of stuff. We talk to imaginary friends. We act out fictional puppet shows. We don't let all the serious day-to-day business of being humans hold us back.

At that age we are still pure. We are experiencing things for the first time. Everything we do is new and exciting, not new and frightening. Our brains are taking in more and more experiences, and we are growing.

As we get older, all the responsibilities we start to deal with begin to overtake this playfulness.

But playfulness is where our most original thinking occurs. The best ideas and breakthrough thinking can come through mucking about and just trying new things.

So, in this book you will find ten weeks of questions all designed to help you unlock your inner creativity.

Questions to inspire kids and adults alike. Whether you're an accountant, a butcher, a singer, a barista, a postal worker, a courier, a shift worker, a lawyer, a student, or a whatever-you-do.

Open-ended questions that you can't just answer 'yes' or 'no' to.

Questions that no two people will answer the same way.

Questions that will unlock your neglected imagination.

All posed by a broad selection of Australia's leading creative minds, from the worlds of art, comedy, literature and advertising.

In ten weeks you will rediscover the inner creative we all have. Because the more often you exercise your creative side, the stronger it will become. And the result will be you'll have a different way of looking at and solving problems at work, at school, and in relationships with your friends and family.

It's part mindfulness, part stupid, part therapy – and part fun.

It's a course designed to help you to think playfully every day. To use your creativity to discover new ways to resolve problems. To put some positivity into the universe. In these turbulent times, if we can get people thinking creatively, we will have a happier world.

So, pick up a pen or pencil. Sharpen your mind. Think outside your day-to-day life, and reconnect with your inner child.

It will be fun. And it might just change the way you think.

let's

go!

week .01

.02

.03

.04

.05

.06

.07

.08

.09

.10

01. population: you

You've just started your own country.
Name it and your new capital city.

my country is

and the capital city is

02. tiny religion

There is a cute village of tiny people that live in your belly button. They make clothing out of lint, use your hair like lumber to build houses, and their main diet consists of dead skin. Three times a week they meet for religious services. What is the focus of their religion?

03. now hiring

Write an advert to encourage people to apply for the position of being you.

04.

doug who?

You spend four hours trapped in a lift wearing nothing except a sock puppet dragon named Doug. How do you explain this to the rescuing firefighters?

05. welcome

Your new colleague is a bear.
What do you suggest for lunch?
Where are you even working?

06. horns up

Draw your surname as a heavy metal logo.

07. planet X

Somewhere between Jupiter and Saturn is an undiscovered planet that is inhabited solely by children. What is it called? How is it different to planet Earth? How is it similar?

stare at a tree swaying in the breeze

week 01. right-brain tip

Studies show that taking a few moments each day to contemplate the magic of everyday things we take for granted can lift our mood and alleviate the stress we gather from worrying about the stuff that weighs us down.

week .02

.01

.03

.04

.05

.06

.07

.08

.09

.10

08. abracadabra

What is the closest thing to real magic? Why?

09. it's a bird, it's a plane . . .

Look up. Describe what you see and why it's important other people see exactly what you do.

10. platy what?

The year is 1797. You are English botanist George Shaw. Describe the platypus for the first time in your letter to Mother England.

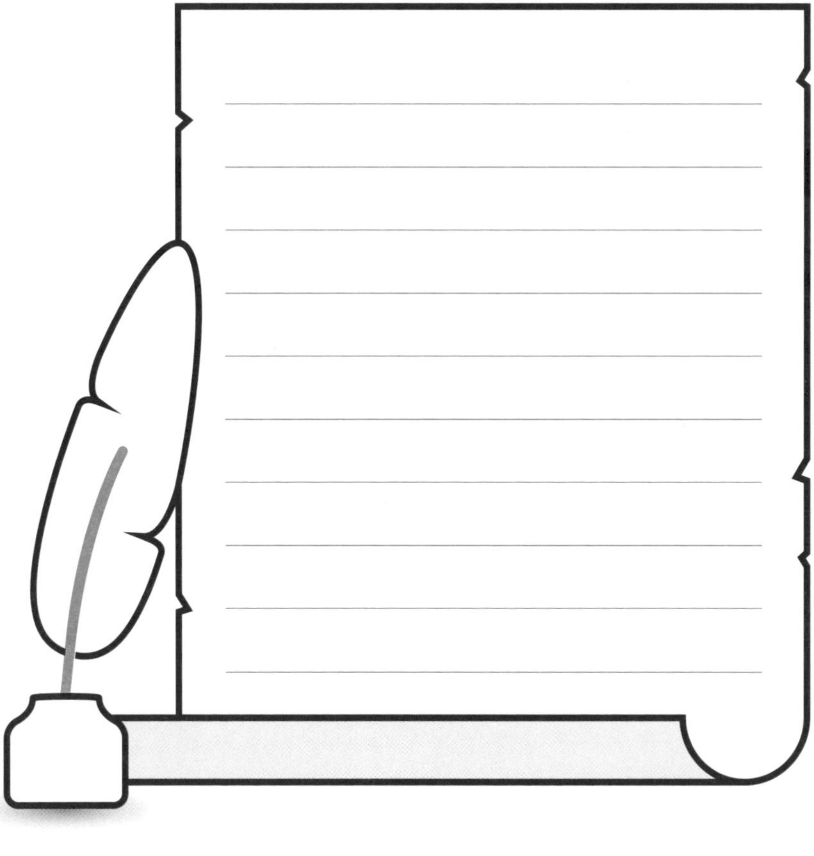

11. slurrrrrp

If you were swallowed by a giant snail, what would it feel like?

12. let's chat

It turns out that plants can actually hear everything, but are sadly mute. Luckily, they feel no pain. What do you think that tree was trying to say to you as you chopped it down last weekend?

13. quote unquote

Can we really take back what we have said?

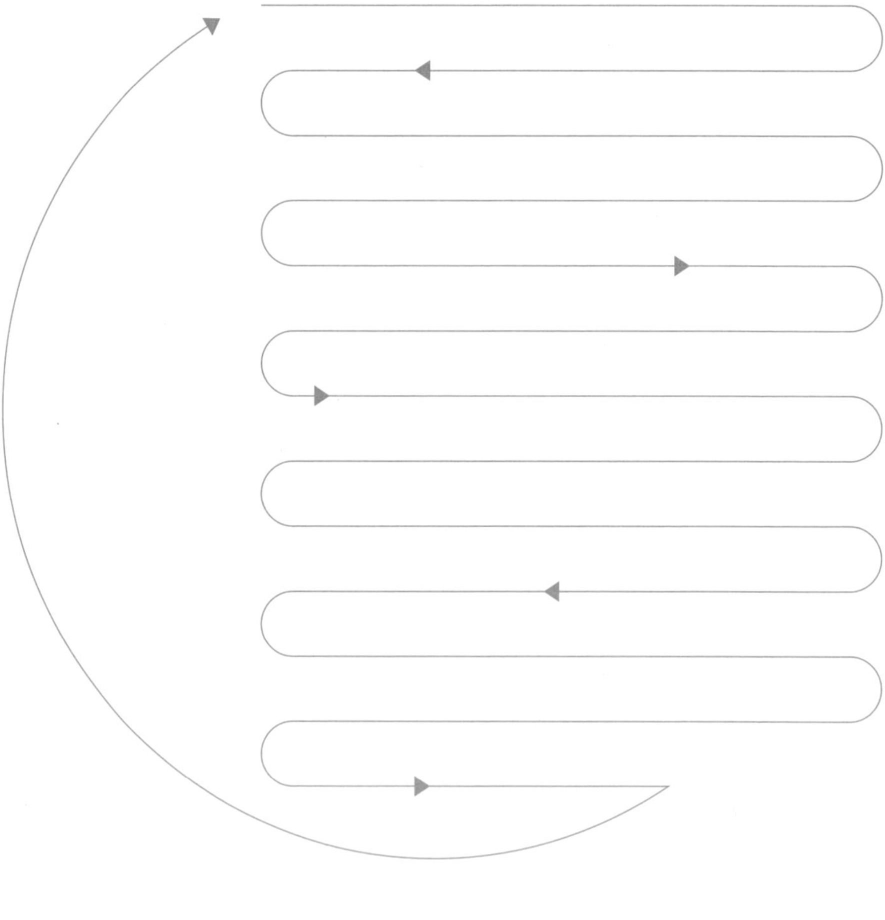

14.

BIG PAGES

RBWO!

battle royal

Invent a superhero and their arch enemy.
What would their first confrontation be about?

VS

read about something you have no interest in

week 02. right-brain tip

By the time we are adults, we have formed some pretty strong opinions. Open your mind up to something you've never heard of, and you just might spark something you've never thought of before.

week .03

15. dancing on the ceiling

Invent a new dance step based on the first piece of furniture that pops into your mind. Describe the moves in detail. Maybe you'll invent 'The Couch', 'The Nightstand' or 'The Table'!

name: ____________________

how: ____________________

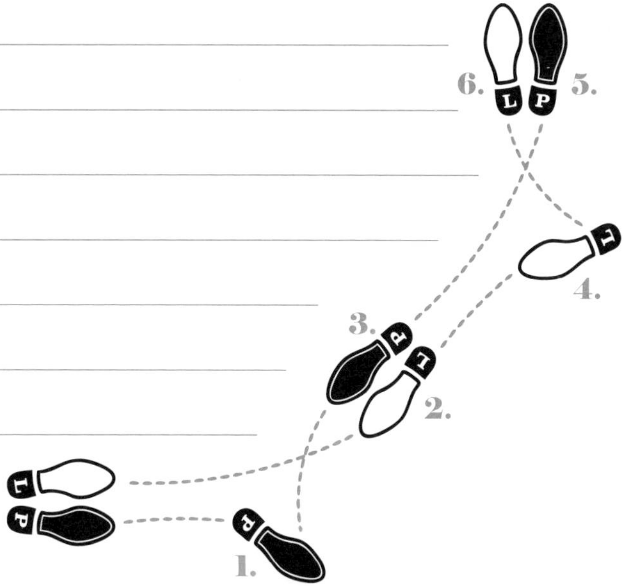

16. paws for thought

Describe what an itch feels like to a puppy.

17. out on a limb

When you hear the wind blow through the leaves of trees, is this the sound of it talking? What does it say?

18. petmoir

If your pet could write an unauthorised, tell-all biography about you, what would its title be? If you don't own a pet, imagine that you own a bandicoot.

19. let's get ready to rumble

If you were a professional wrestler, what would be your ring name, and what would be your gimmick? Describe the finishing move that you would use to win the world title.

name

finishing move

20. shock tv

If you could host a TV show, what would it be called and why would it be pulled off air during the first episode?

21. hermie the love crab

Imagine you're not a dog person or a cat person, but a hermit crab person. Convince someone to be a hermit crab person, too.

sweat at least five times a week

week 03. right-brain tip

'Healthy body, healthy mind.'
It's a cliché for a reason. Because it's true. When you exercise, your body releases endorphins that make you feel good. And when you feel good, anything's possible.

week .04

.01
.02
.03
.05
.06
.07
.08
.09
.10

22. i'll have ten

Think of ten new words that could mean 'sausage'.

1.
2.
3.
4.
5.
6.
7.
8.
9.
10.

23. mini me

If you could time-travel and meet yourself as a child, what would you say to yourself to prove who you were?

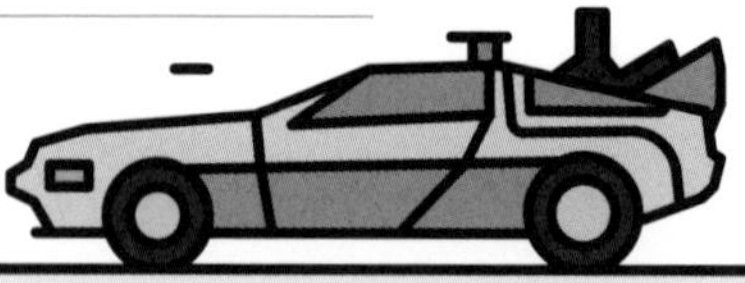

24. bad to worse

List all the things that are wrong with your life and devise ways to make each of them even worse.

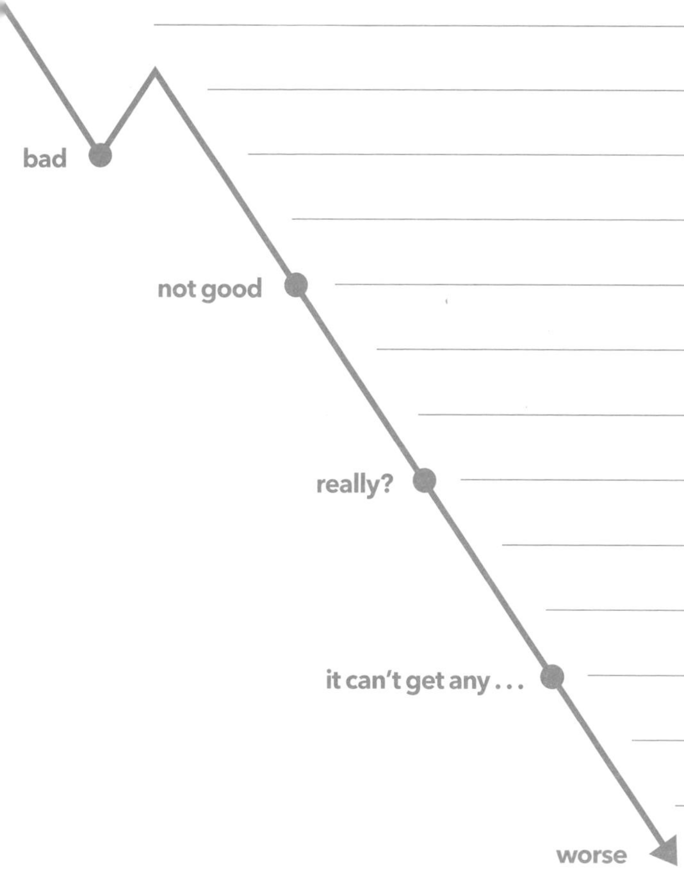

25. fine feathered friend

Write a short story about a homing pigeon named Bert.

26. five for one

Dolphins sleep with one eye open.
Think of five reasons why.

1.1

1.2

1.3

1.4

1.5

27. sock-less monster

There's a creature that steals all our socks from the washing. Draw it.

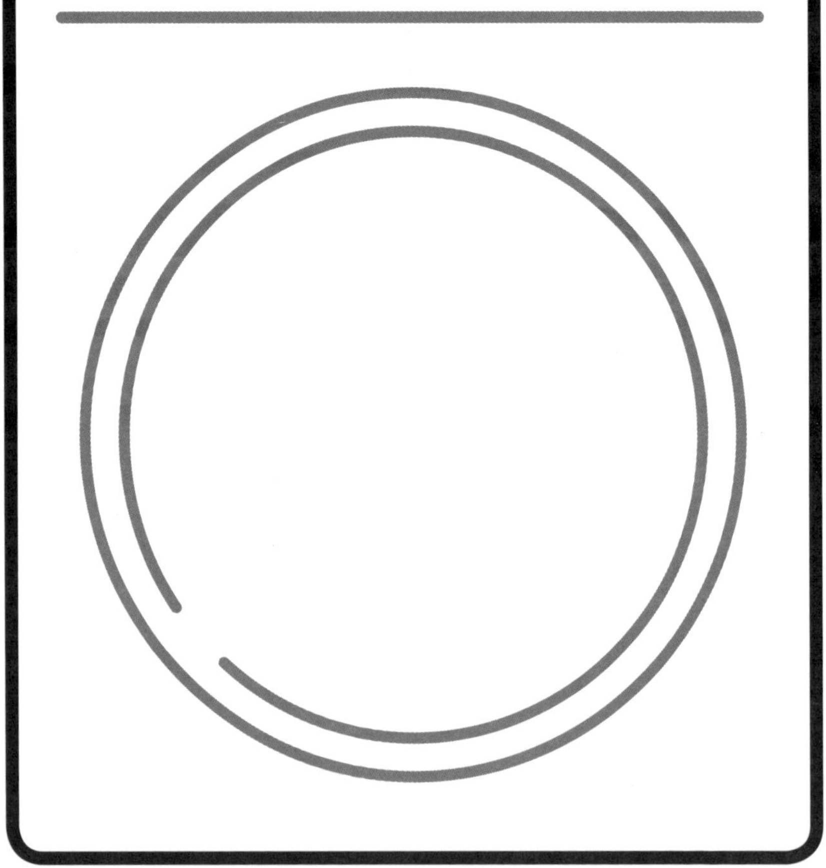

28. mmmmm, inedible

Invent a new breakfast cereal that excludes anything edible. Create a name and catchphrase for it.

listen to the sound of your heart beating

week 04. right-brain tip

Silence can awaken your brain. Doing one thing at a time is something we all too rarely do nowadays. The sound of your heart beating might remind you that every moment is precious. Try it tonight.

week .05

.01
.02
.03
.04
.06
.07
.08
.09
.10

29. show me the money

In twenty years' time, after Botox has faded from the market because of a major botulism outbreak, what will be the new miracle to halt ageing? Describe why hosts of morning TV shows will love it.

30. trio of dips

Invent a new sport to be played by three teams.

what:

how:

31. let down

As a kid, what did you think would be awesome about being an adult, but actually isn't? Why?

32. blended pup

What would you call a breed of dog whose father was a Bulldog and mother was a Shih tzu?

33. in a spin

If a tornado had feelings, what do you think they would be?

34. bounced

A vampire, a werewolf and a demon walk into a bar, but the bouncer blocks the door and points to the 'NO DOGS ALLOWED' sign. How do they talk their way in?

35. don't be cross

Other than zebra, what crossings would be useful to humans, and why?

get eight hours sleep every night

week 05. right-brain tip

The average person is only getting around six hours and forty minutes of sleep each night. It simply isn't enough to function at your best. So, hit the hay earlier and wake up with a clearer mind.

week .06

36. top of the pops

Write the first verse to your hit song,
'I married a mushroom so just deal with it, Dad!'

37. rubbish trip

Close your eyes. Imagine you're visiting your nearest rubbish dump. Find something useful, take it home, clean it, and use it. Now describe your day like it's the most inspiring day of your life.

38. dead funny

Think of the funniest thing you could do or say on your death bed.

39. nice pear

If an apple a day keeps the doctor away,
what does a pear a day keep away?

40. C.C.C.

Write a convincing argument about why cake is racist in fewer than sixty-five words.

41. butcher but not

What would a butcher that only does cuts of vegetables be called?

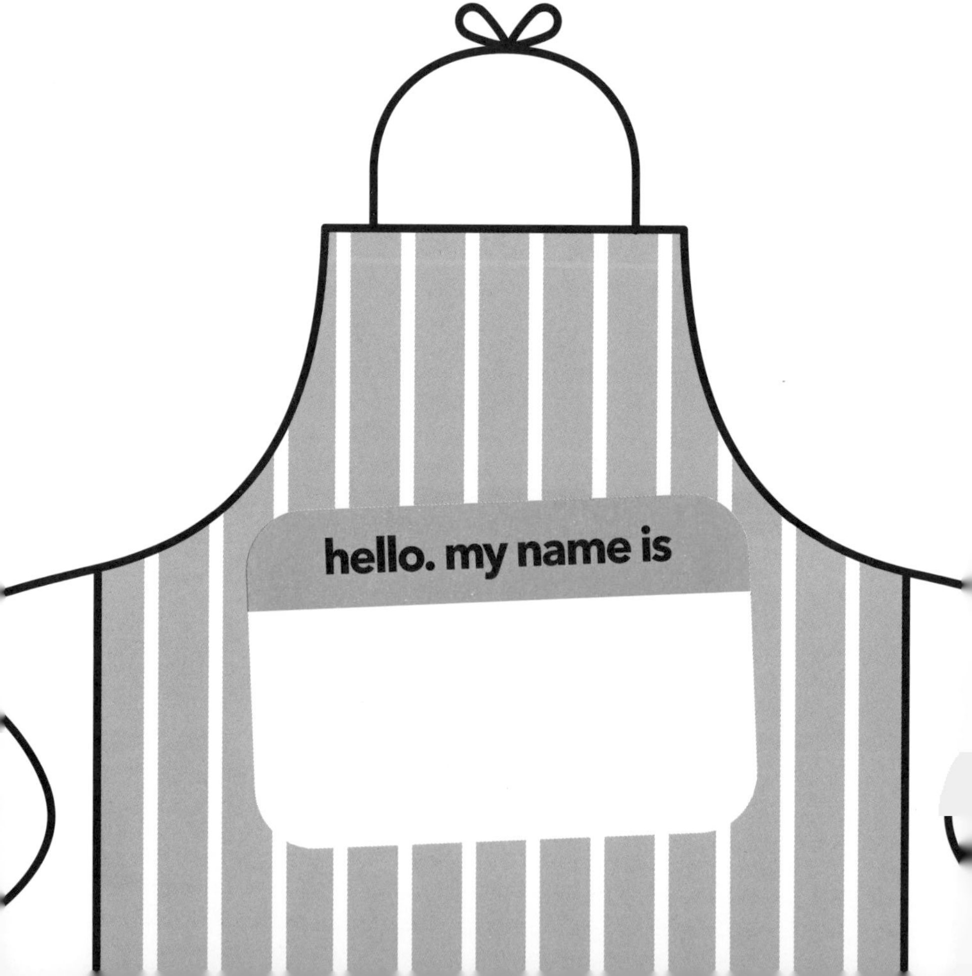

42. to the left, to the left

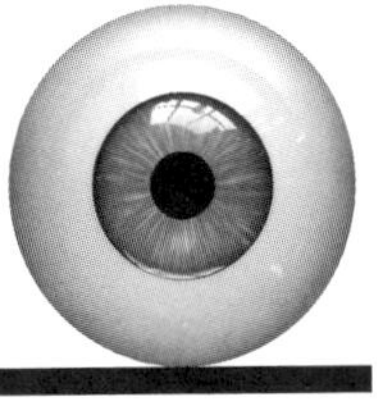

Describe a loved-one's left eye.

cut out sugar

week 06. right-brain tip

Consuming sugar stimulates the release of the mood-boosting neurotransmitter serotonin. Constantly over-activating these serotonin pathways with more sugar can deplete our limited supplies of the chemical, which can contribute to symptoms of depression. Keep a clear head. Clear out the sugar.

week .07

.01
.02
.03
.04
.05
.06

.08
.09
.10

43. where do I start

What's wrong with people?

44. colour blind

Draw the colour red using only a blue pen.

45. Wow

A hippo and an earthworm have a baby.
Write a Wikipedia entry about it.

name: ____________________

46. big rock

If the moon wasn't The Moon, what should it be called and how would you sell it as a tourist attraction?

47. do the robot

If your childhood best friend told you he or she was a robot built by aliens one hundred years ago, what would you do?

48. rewind ◂◂

Choose the last movie you hated.
Write a better ending.

49. meow and then

Describe a dream a cat might have about secretly wanting to be a dog.

tune out the news

week 07. right-brain tip

We live in an age of information overload. Life is 24/7, and it's easy to get caught up in watching distracting videos or scrolling through social media. Try putting that time into something you feel passionate about that will have a tangible impact. You'll free up a big chunk of time instantly.

week .08

.01
.02
.03
.04
.05
.06
.07
.09
.10

50. full on

If a comet crashed into the sun and only left us with half a sun, and half the light, how would the world be different?

51. way back when

Think of your earliest memory.
Write down what you think happened
just before that.

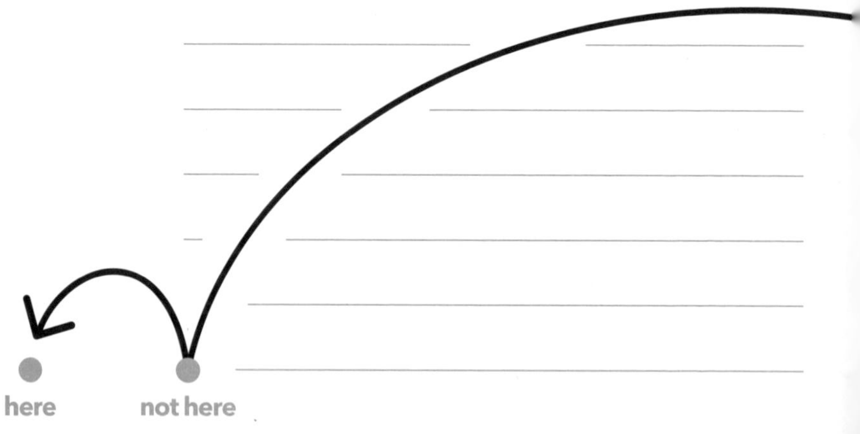

52. go go gadget

Design a shoe that could help you climb up the side of a ship in a storm.

53. reel time

Imagine you are watching a time-lapse movie of your entire life. What stands out? What is the accompanying soundtrack?

54. uber healthy

If clay was discovered to be a new superfood, what would it be renamed for consumers?

55. and on the seventh day

If people believe in God,
what does a Dog believe in?

56. open home

How would you persuade a homeowner to invite a homeless person to live in the spare bedroom for six months?

spend five minutes inside a church in the city

week 08. right-brain tip

Churches are quiet. And often empty. They can be places of solitude to reflect and recharge. You don't have to believe in God or be religious to feel the overwhelming quiet – a quiet that is a world away from the busy noise inside your mind.

.01

.02

.03

.04

.05

.06

.07

.08

week .09

.10

57. one small step

Do ants always run, always walk, or always jog? Describe a race between the members of a colony of ants.

START

FINISH

58. trip advisor

When travelling through the Amazon rainforest in only your socks and underpants, would you take a machete or a cigarette lighter as your only tool? Why?

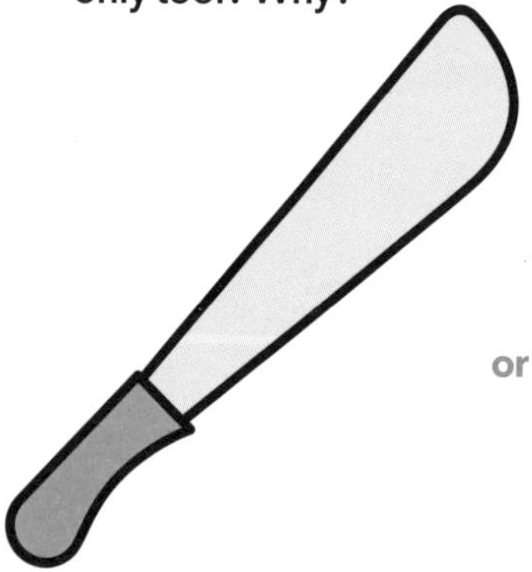

or

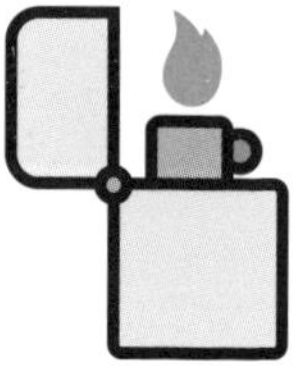

why: ______________________________

____

____

____

____

____

____

59. nudie run

You've been arrested for public nudity.
Give your version of events to the judge.

60. sticky situation

How would you explain facial expressions to an alien with tentacles instead of a face?

61. jump to it

Write a poem about a kangaroo covered in tattoos who likes to liberate animals from zoos. Then send it to Australia's Prime Minister at www.pm.gov.au/contact-your-pm

62. greetings

You know that moment when someone says 'hello' and you respond 'good, thanks'? Give that moment an actual name and describe how it feels.

hello

good, thanks

name: ______________________________

feels like: ______________________________

63. seventh heaven

Think of seven soups that no-one in human history has thought of before, and that would be quite nice to eat.

1.

2.

3.

4.

5.

6.

7.

read more

week 09. right-brain tip

Sitting alone by yourself reading is one of life's great pleasures – a pleasure we often deny ourselves because we are too busy. Make the time to open yourself up to experiencing life from an angle you haven't considered.

.01

.02

.03

.04

.05

.06

.07

.08

.09

week .10

64. warning label

The label on this jar of jam says 'Not for External Use'. Give us the brief outline of events that led to it being necessary for the jam company to print that on the label.

65. humaning

If aliens were to drop lines from the sky to catch humans like we catch fish, what would be the best bait?

66. hello

If you weren't allowed to mention your work, what would you say if someone asked you 'what do you do?'

someone: **what do you do?**

you: ______________________________

67. not a word more

Describe in exactly thirty-seven words what the most inspiring thing was in the room you were last in.

68. sweeeeeeet

Think of a new name for a doughnut.

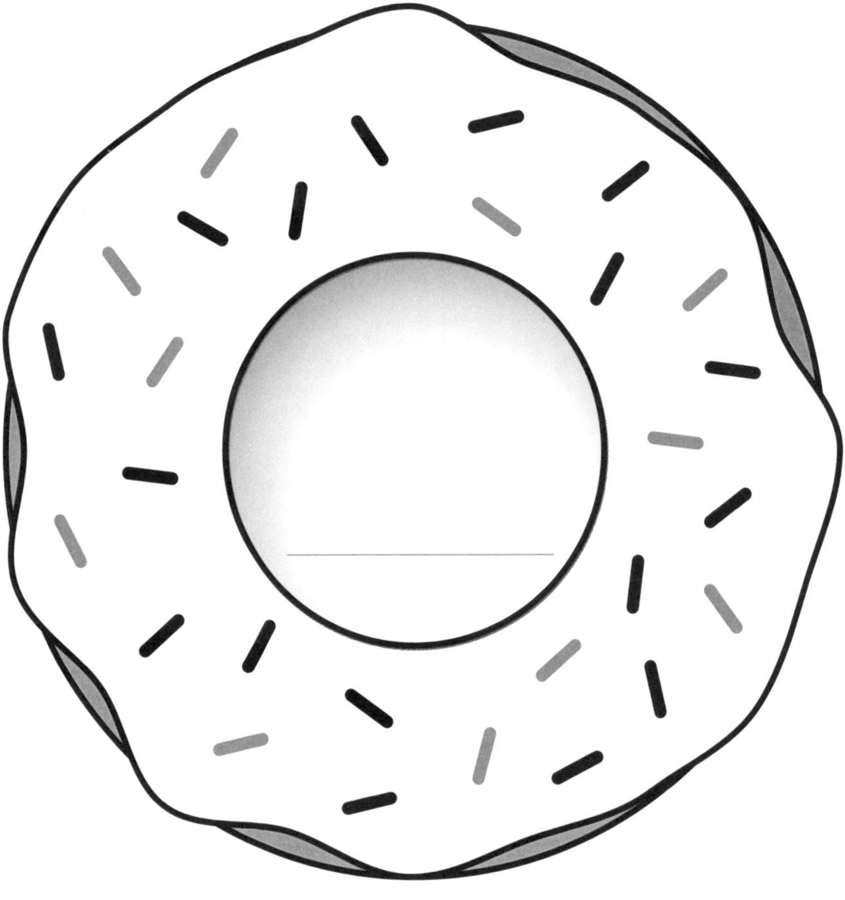

69. in its unnatural habitat

Different breeds of dogs have sex with each other, just like cats do. But birds stick to their own kind. Invent the best bird crossbreed you can think of and describe how David Attenborough would talk about it.

70. a call to arms

If you were a tiny plastic figurine, what two tiny plastic accessories would you come with?

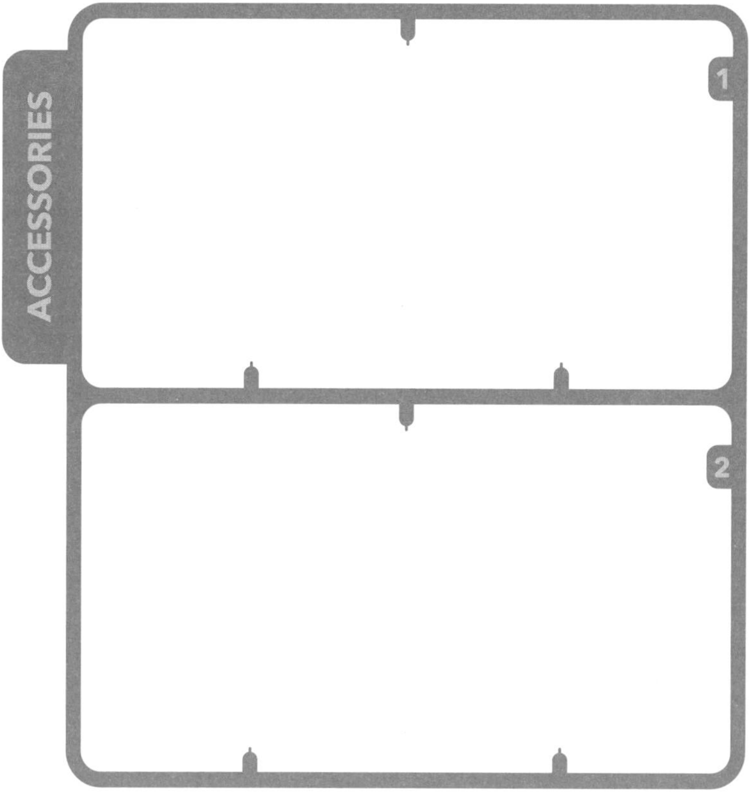

look at a cloud

week 10. right-brain tip

As a kid, did you ever lie on the grass and just look at the clouds? What objects did you see? No doubt it was a calming experience. Being at one with nature has a way of rewiring the human brain to see possibilities otherwise overlooked. So, find a spot of grass and reawaken your inner child. It just might help you look at problems with a new perspective.

well

done

so, how does your brain feel now?

Ten weeks.

Seventy questions.

And seventy different ways to get your brain working outside the box.

now what?

Hopefully you've enjoyed exercising your creative side over the last seventy days.

With any luck, you'll have accessed a part of your brain that is fun, interesting and positive. Proving that being creative is not all about painting pictures and being a starved, tortured artist.

Being creative means solving problems and thinking about things from a fresh angle.

Being creative means not settling for doing things the way they've always been done.

Being creative means having time out from shiny objects that take our focus off the best things in life.

And the best thing about being creative is that anyone can do it.

So, now take this new-found creativity and apply it.

to your work.

to your relationships.

to your play.

Whenever there's a problem that's proving tough to crack, turn to your right side.

You never know what you might come up with.

the right-brain brains trust

This book couldn't have happened without the wonderful contributions from the following creative legends. Many thanks to all of them who donated their brains to pose the curly questions in *The Right-brain Workout*.

Questions 1 & 39 - Brian Thacker
Brian is the author of seven books, including *Rule No. 5: No Sex on the Bus (confessions of a tour leader), Planes, Trains & Elephants* and (2009 Travel Book of the Year) *Sleeping Around*. He's also a travel journalist and advertising art director.
brianthacker.tv

Questions 2 & 64 - Steven Nicholson
Steven is a multidisciplinary creative, who works in the fields of technology, animation, direction, and creating things that are impossible to create. He's won advertising's highest accolade (a Cannes Grand Prix) amongst many others.
airbag.co

Questions 3 & 70 - Darby Hudson
Darby is one of Australia's foremost modern poets. He's been published in *Best Australian Poems*, *Meanjin* and *Cordite*, as well as writing and illustrating the books *Walk* and *Picture Songs*. An anthology of his work has been published by Five Islands Press.
darbyhudson.com

Questions 4 & 34 - Brendon Guthrie
Brendon is a freelance writer and one-time advertising creative director at advertising agencies DDB, J Walter Thompson and Ogilvy.

Questions 5 & 48 – Rob Stephens

Rob is a musician, audio engineer and sound designer. By day he records, produces sound design, and composes music out of Bang Bang Studios (Melbourne), Soundbyte Studios (WA), and as a freelancer. By night, he performs and writes music with a variety of musical projects.

bangbangstudios.com.au

Question 6 – Ben Couzens

Ben is the co-founder and co-executive creative director of Melbourne advertising agency Thinkerbell. He's also the lead guitarist in murder-fuzz rock merchants Mammoth Mammoth.

thinkerbell.com

mammothmammoth.com

Questions 7 & 45 – Kimmie Neidhart

Kimmie founded creative agency Burd, and likes to use her insight and skill for good.

burd.com.au

Question 8 – Luisa Paine

Luisa is an artist, art director and creative director. With twenty years' experience collaborating in advertising, fashion, art and design, she works as an independent creative.

luisapaine.com

Question 9 – Dmitri Golovko

Dmitri is an award-winning music composer and sound designer with more than ten years' experience creating music and sound for films, TV shows, commercials and games. His music has been featured in films such as 2017's *The Hitman's Bodyguard*, the 2018 Netflix show *Pine Gap*, as well as the recent series *Ms Fisher's Modern Murder Mysteries*.

dgmusic.tv

Question 10 - Karen Ferry
Karen is an advertising creative and regular panellist on ABC TV's *Gruen*. Internationally awarded and recognised, she is also the national co-Head of AWARD School (The Australasian Writers and Art Directors Association), Australia's leading portfolio school for junior creatives.
karenferry.com

Question 11 - John Akritidis
John is a partner in independent advertising and communications agency Marmalade. His work for Beyond Blue has helped reshape how Australians look at mental health.
marmalademelbourne.com

Question 12 - Nick Cummins
Nick is creative partner at The Royals, the self-proclaimed World's Most Interested Agency.
theroyals.com

Questions 13 - Thom Rigney
Thom is a Melbourne-based photographer with a penchant for portraying the untold narratives that underlie the unassuming and eclectic characters and landscapes around us. The aim being to create original and authentic work.
thomrigney.com

Questions 14 & 42 - Ben Akers
Ben is the founder of MADE WITH +, a problem-solving collective of writers, directors, designers, producers and artists that create work good for the world. His feature-length documentary *Steve*, about male depression and suicide, is currently going where the men are - and touring pubs around the world.
stevedocumentary.com

Question 15 - David Ponce de León
David is the executive creative director of Ogilvy Melbourne. He has previously been head of AWARD School Melbourne.

Questions 16 & 46 – Adam White
Adam is an award-winning filmmaker from Melbourne. Following a career as a professional footballer, he shifted his focus to filmmaking, and his short films have screened at Telluride, SXSW, Clermont Ferrand and HBO Comedy Arts Festival. His debut feature film, *Lone Wolf*, stars Hugo Weaving and Tilda Cobham-Hervey.
futurepictures.tv

Question 17 – Paul Meates
Paul is a part-time artist, full-time creative director and long-time dad. For the first two visit **wasnotme.com**

Question 18 – Bill Irving
Bill is a Melbourne-based filmmaker and commercials director. His documentary feature film, *Watan*, was released in 2018.
billirving.com.au

Questions 19 & 27 – Angus Loxton
Angus is a copywriter at Wunderman Thompson in Sydney. In just a few years he has worked at some of Australia's most creative advertising agencies and in 2019 he was awarded a spot on B&T's 30 Under 30 list.
loxtoncreative.com

Questions 20 & 61 – Tom Whitty
Tom is an award-winning journalist, TV producer and social justice campaigner. When he's not making TV, he's making music . . . for TV.
circustreesounds.com

Question 21 – Shannon Crowe
Shannon is an idea thinker, creative writer and alpha mama. She is one of the world's most awarded advertising copywriters, passionate university lecturers and proudest advocates of equality within the advertising industry.
shannoncrowecreative.com

Questions 22 & 51 – Antony Simmons
Antony is a senior art director at Clemenger BBDO. Previously he was creative director at design firm Elmwood, and launched Australia's first boxed water, Do Water.

Questions 23 & 53 – Hayden Gregory
Hayden is an award-winning filmmaker and multidisciplinary artist based in Melbourne.
haydengregory.com

Questions 24 & 63 – Paul Foot
Paul is an international comedian who studied mathematics at Oxford University. He discovered comedy by accident and immediately rethought his plans to become an accountant. Paul regularly tours the UK, Australia, Canada, the US and Europe, and is known for his unique, idiosyncratic stage presence and innovative and surrealist comedy.
paulfoot.tv

Question 25 – Stu Morley
Stu is a creative photographer and cinematographer working in and around fashion and advertising. He is also the managing director of the photography space Disco Studios in St Kilda, Melbourne.
stumorley.com

Question 26 – Paul Taylor
Paul is one of Australia's most respected advertising creative directors. In his thirty-year career he helped M&C Saatchi to be the number one creative agency in Australia. He is now a social impact entrepreneur whose work for Bank Australia has put the Big Four on notice.

Question 28 – Ryan Clayton
Ryan is a senior art director and designer with over thirteen years' experience in advertising. He is currently developing an animated adult sitcom called *Rezzies*. He has also tutored at AWARD School.
ryanclayton.com

Questions 29 & 60 – Jess Gunn
Jess is a copywriter based in Amsterdam. She has created campaigns for Australian clients including L'Oréal Paris, Maybelline, Metro Trains, AGL and Tigerair; and international brands Coca-Cola, Netflix and Heineken.
jessgunn.com

Question 30 – Waleed Aly
Waleed is a broadcaster, writer and academic. He loves sport, music, travel and Batman, and will do anything to make work incorporate them.

Question 31 – Emma Robbins
Emma is one of the most highly decorated copywriters in Australia. She is currently executive creative director of M&C Saatchi Melbourne.

Question 32 – Paul Carpenter
Paul is an art director by day, and creator of things that appeal to the right side of the brain. One of his creative distractions is turning your pet photos into old master oil paintings. Celebrity clients have included Dr Chris Brown, Kate Langbroek, Amanda Keller and Dave Hughes.
www.pompouspets.com

Question 33 – Annie Egan
Annie is an associate creative director at R/GA, New York. Passionate about unique and original storytelling across all media, Annie has extensive experience creating and producing integrated campaigns for brands in the US and Australia. Her work includes the social experiment, Very Worst Very Best, where she asks people on the streets of New York, London and Melbourne about their very worst and their very best moments.
annieegan.com

Question 35 – Nicholas Bufalo
Nicholas Bufalo has more than thirty years' experience in the Australian entertainment industry, ranging from acting to writing to directing. He has directed TV shows such as *Packed to the Rafters*, *City Homicide*, *All Saints* and *Winners and Losers*.

Questions 36 & 62 – Tommy Little
Tommy is a comedian and dispenser of the finest dickheadery.
tommylittle.com.au

Question 37 – Billy Plummer
Billy is an ad-agency creative-director-turned-photographer with a deliberately distinctive style. His work is all about revealing the extraordinary in the ordinary.
billyplummer.com

Question 38 – Luke Thompson
Luke is a creative director at Australia's most successful advertising agency, Clemenger BBDO. He's worked for a number of advertising agencies around the globe, and his campaign for Tourism Victoria's Melbourne Remote Control Tourist was accepted into New York's MoMA collection.
lukethompsonwork.com

Question 40 – Ali Berg
Ali is creative director and co-founder of Hedgehog Agency. She is also the author of *The Book Ninja* and *While You Were Reading*, books inspired by her Books on the Rail project, which encourages people to leave the book they've been reading on the train for someone else to enjoy.
hedgehogagency.com.au
booksontherail.com
aliandmichelle.com

Question 41 – Dave Gibson
Dave is the co-founder of Hawke's Brewing Co., a beer company created in conjunction with former Australian Prime Minister Bob Hawke.
hawkesbrewing.com

Questions 43 & 59 – Josh Robbins
Josh is a Melbourne-based visual artist. Predominantly a painter, his varied body of work is in part inspired by the natural environment, and includes typographic works, portraiture and conceptual pieces. Josh has exhibited throughout Australia and the UK.
joshrobbins.com

Question 44 – Michael Farr
Michael is a UI designer at men's health charity movement Movember. He has raised tens of thousands of dollars for men's mental health with his Tour de Parma cycle between Sydney and Melbourne, on which he has chats about mental health with men over a parma in the country towns along the way.
www.tourdeparma.com

Question 47 – Josh Logue
Josh is one of Australia's best-looking freelance comedy and VFX directors, who carved out a career in the design space before moving into music video directing, live action and animation.
joshlogue.com

Question 49 – Ellie Dunn
Ellie is a copywriter and a drummer in Melbourne indie rock band Dark Fair, who are signed to Poison City Records.

Question 50 – Ed Bechervaise
Ed is a creative strategist and creative director at The Icon Agency, and a practising abstract artist under his street-artist pseudonym, Unwell Bunny. He has had eight solo shows in Melbourne and Paris.
unwellbunny.com
frictioncreativethinking.com

Question 52 – Alex Wadelton
Alex is one of Australia's most respected advertising minds. He has raised hundreds of thousands of dollars for charities with an array of campaigns. He's also good at writing in the third person.
stuffbyalexwadelton.com

Question 54 – Fiona McLeod
Fiona is a graphic designer at BMF Advertising in Sydney and has worked in many design disciplines in the UK and Australia. She is passionate about branding, advertising and solving problems through conceptual design solutions.
fionamcleod.com.au

Question 55 – Craig Griffin

Craig began his film career directing and producing music videos for leading Australian artists. He has gone on to produce television commercials and feature-length documentaries including *Not Quite Hollywood*, *Such Is Life: The Troubled Times of Ben Cousins* and *First Love*, and wrote, produced and directed *Uncharted Waters*. He is based in Melbourne and runs the production company The Directors Group.

directorsgroup.com.au

Question 56 – Nigel Dawson

Nigel has spent all his working life in advertising agencies both large and small, local and multinational, from London to Hong Kong to Melbourne. Somewhat prematurely, he was given a Lifetime Achievement Award a few years ago, though he continues to try to achieve results for clients through his partnership, Three Wise Men.

three-wise-men.com.au

Question 57 – Christopher Tovo

Christopher is a photographer, director and cinematographer. He has shot all around the world for clients such as the AFL, Schweppes, Tennis Australia, Westpac and many more.

christophertovo.com

Question 58 – Tom Franks

Tom is an engineer-turned-advertising-image-maker whose dynamic and atmospheric images have seen him create distinctive print campaigns across Europe, Asia and Australia for the last decade.

tomfranksphoto.com

Question 65 – Huei Yin Wong

Huei is an art director who wrote her question completely sober. Whether calling out environmental apathy with her Pantone Colour of the Year: Bleached Coral project, or thinking up new names for restaurants (Boom Shaka Laksa, anyone?), she always exercises her right brain – it's the only exercise she does.

heyhuei.com

Question 66 – Frank Trobbiani
Frank is a writer, art director, illustrator, designer and drummer in murder-fuzz rock merchants Mammoth Mammoth.
mammothmammoth.com

Question 67 – Josh Frizzell
Josh is a director living and working in New Zealand. Coming from a music video and commercial background has given him a fresh eye in the world of drama. He was nominated as Best Director for a Drama at the 2017 New Zealand Television Awards for his work on *The Brokenwood Mysteries*.
frizzell.tv

Question 68 – Kim Hellier
Kim is a designer and art director who works at behaviour-change communications agency The Shannon Company, and has worked at various local and international agencies over many years. In between she has completed a Masters in Communication Design at RMIT and reared two children.

Question 69 – Steve Callen
Steve is an award-winning writer and film director. Currently, Steve writes and directs film projects for clients, ad agencies and production companies directly, both in Australia and all over the world. When he's not creating ads, he continues to develop his own projects for both film and television.
stevecallen-director.com
www.stevecallen-writer.com
www.stevecallen.com

acknowledgements

Russel Howcroft

Being the Chair of the Australian Film, Television and Radio School (AFTRS) has inspired me to aggressively pursue the importance of creativity for all Australians. The executive team at AFTRS has supported me in the development of the arguments as to why this is so important for all of us. And for that, I sincerely thank them.

My partners at PwC have been incredible in their support for the role of creative thinking in society.

Thanks to the ABC and production team at CJZ.

And finally to the most creative cats I know: Kate, Claudia, Charlie and Louis.

Alex Wadelton

Massive thanks to the following who inspire me on a daily basis:

Darby Hudson for illuminating life from a different angle. Tom Whitty for inspiring me to do better things for the world. Aaron Tyler for keeping on keeping on. Tanya Hosch for being a force of nature. Tommy Little for being the best comedian-cum-model I know. Stu Morley for his Ryan Reynolds impersonations and completing the crew that means a lot to me. Bill Shannon for proving that you can use advertising for good every day. Alex Lopez for showing me what a decent human being really is. Paul Chapman for inspiring three flags for the Cats. :) The Joe Rogan and Tim Ferriss podcasts for introducing me to a whole range of different ways of thinking and living. Shea Serrano for convincing me (and thousands more) to 'shoot my shot'. Nikki Christer, Clive Hebard and Adam Laszczuk from Penguin Random House for believing in the idea and making it look so good. Russel for turning a pipe dream into an exciting reality.

And, of course, most importantly, to my wonderful family of the brilliant Sheridan, Roarke the rocket, and the magical Princess Lila, for always believing in me and all of my crazy ideas. I wouldn't be here today if it wasn't for you.